somewhere

between

shadow and

light

somewhere
between shadow and light

---

mariesa faer

SMOKEBLOOD PUBLISHING

Casper, WY

SMOKEBLOOD

somewhere between shadow and light

@mariesa_faer

ISBN-13: 978-0-9600491-1-0

Published by Smokeblood Publishing
Casper, WY | smokeblood.com

Cover design © Smokeblood 2019

First Edition

Printed in the United States of America

somewhere between
shadow and light

a soul grows

unfurling amidst the elements
a soul comes to know
itself

somewhere between
shadow and light

to those who
held the shards of my shattered soul together
while I glued through spicy tears

walked me through my nightmares
and stood still beside
as I screamed away the pains
of a lost heart

this is for you

elements :

shadow

between

light

shadow

darkness builds
it builds up all around

if you let it
and you don't check it

it will try to take you down

I sleep
in the belly
of a great battle

sometimes
the sniggers
sights and stories of living
sneak in
and shake me awake

greeting my adjusting eyes
with a tease of tension
like a frozen hide
on damp dormant skin

INSOMNIA

I drink and smoke
and poke all around
inside my mouth

a futile attempt
to relieve a tension
I wrote for myself

IF ONLY I COULD FIND THE ERASER

there's a tightness
in my chest
tugging from throat to navel
calling on me to address
what makes my soul unravel

SOMATIC SIGNS

my anxieties
fill up my mind
and cause me to forget
all the time
as it passes
beneath the shadows
of my eyes

DISTRACTIONS

I see the denial
behind their eyes

they watch through blindness
as my spirit cries

I can't
keep saying no forever

so I'll go

– create some distance –

to avoid
breaking the hearts that hold
me too close
and suffocate without seeing
the pain they cause
from too much dependence

what they mistake
as freeing

CODEPENDENCY

I'd slice off my sadness
goose bump by goose bump
but would you notice the scars
or just presume I have
cat scratches on
my forearms

S E L F - H A T E

my woman parts ache in anticipation
for the pain they have inherited

for goddess' sake
I'd like another
I'm on a dating prohibition

I've got vagina splinters from all the
bad wood I've been working
in the shop

oh I know I can please you
just gimme a minute
to adjust myself
to make you happy
to make you feel
how I know you like to

with the lightest
the slightest touch I can
force the good stuff
while I hide myself behind
our intimacy

the stairs jump around
before my fuming eyes

my vision shaking
the ground quaking

beneath your piles of lies

FIGHTS

I slept in the snow
last night

still

it was warmer
than being with you

RESENTMENT

swat me away
like a fly
too many times
and I just might die

DISREGARD

do emotions like this
kill you
can emotions this strong
take you down

?

HOW AM I STILL HERE

CORTISOL

darkness and light sometimes
confuse themselves
behind
my eyelids
at night
as
this slow
creeping thing
that haunts me
while I dream
refuses to decide
if I will survive
or take myself down
before the next sunrise

my hyper – awareness
lay over me like a film

a dewy
glassy
peeling film

sure
I stretch it and
tug at it and
peel some of it off

yet it lies there

prohibiting
what could be
greatness

even when I'm driving
all alone in my car
the anxiety comes creeping in

it's never off too far

and I wonder
what would be left of me
without this anxiety

FREEDOM

the possibility of failure
trumped the option for success
so once we looked around
there was no more hope left

what's left
after the dreams
have faded
and they're all
worn out
by a world that doesn't love them

R E S I D U E

time pulls me around
like I have no say
no control
in where I go

stringing me along

it has taken my right to consent

can I get
anywhere at all
in this way
dragged around by numbers
day after day

I search for meaning
for I'm not at peace

TURMOIL

my ribs just collapsed
into a pile of dust

they couldn't support the
size of my heart there for a second

and maybe
just not anymore

COLLAPSE

matcha in the morning
and golden milk at night
yes I love my body
and you shoulda known I was gonna fight

wide – eyed in old places
where I once lost my self
I turn back now
but only
to configure my new health

yes you fucked up big time
when you took my silence as consent
yes I think you're still redeemable
but there's not many second chances
you haven't already spent

yeah they say most female cancer patients
had sexual abuse in their history
and a wish to die
buried ever just so deeply down inside

one does not exist without the other
we've got to change the cultural disorder

now
I know myself
and I love myself
more than I even know

but you and that darkness in darkness
attached these cells of self-hate
for my body
to start to grow

and yes in our party culture
I'm supposed to say
it's okay
it's no big deal
happens all the time

but motherfucker
that's not real

it was a big giant deal
for the girl who woke up
and wasn't alone

for the girl who had to wake up
to the harsh realities of the world
in one damning fell swoop
on All Hallow's Eve
when her inner trust
became unfurled
and was taken
and was swirled
by a man who'd chosen deceit

DYSPLASIA

I could claw the tears
from under my eyes

rippling and ripping
the opaque skies

a sadness like this
could bleed someone
like you
dry

– watch out –

taking all you are
with an overwhelming cry

BEWARE

this love is homesickness
and all I can write
is seemingly
what I know

what limitations
of self – induced incarcerations

where are my tried and true
illusionary practices
now
where's the bloody
creativity here

for opening
past the pain

when immersed
within the borders
of my own
emotionally
distressed
little brain

LIMITATIONS OF PERCEPTION

I cannot believe
I let you in

let you hold me
all night

only for you to wake up
turn around
and cut me down
with every tool on your belt
telling me fake stories
to defend your case
against my role
in this place

you didn't get what you wanted
well here's a surprise
for you
neither did I
but I've started to learn
over time
to love the beasts inside
I'm disappointed
to say the very least
that you can be so cold and cruel
and not even see that this has all
just been
oh just all about you
but then

cut me down
go about your day
act like nothing ever happened
like you didn't just rip out each
every one of my characteristics
and backdrop execute them

tell them all
they're pieces of shit
then walk away
leaving me with it
disheveled
and scattered
around this house
we try to call a home

but I feel drenched in fear
each time I hear
you coming back here
to this place
where I let myself be vulnerable

I guess
it's my fault

for letting you in at all

A VENGEANCE

I shiver between shelters
avoiding the screams inside my soul
that try to tell me to stop moving
that I've got nowhere left to go

OVERUSED OPPORTUNITIES

you take your time avoiding
to the point where you're exhausted and
overworked and
eventually give up
get sick
and say *I'll try again next time*

ending lives like
placing bookmarks
in experiential growth

scared of ourselves
scared of everything

unable to see the greater truth

I come from a world of manipulative bitches
and it can be hard to rise above
choosing something else
when it seems they're living life
the easy way
– path of least resistance
kinda stuff –
but
they are only fooling themselves
(much like I have done)
and hurt others along the way
coaxing themselves into thinking
that they're full of loving kindness
but in the reality
they are just pretty enough
not to get caught
in their own nets
of bullshits

INTERWOVEN WEBS

life is this horrible
little thing
we whittle our way through
like being born
buried alive
in a cold
crevasse of a cave
way deep inside
given only
a screwdriver
with which to carve
through the space
to find our way
to light

do you lose
all you've gained
when you shift again

?

ACCUMULATION

we are all
so wounded by this world
so molded by the state
of our over – sexualization
and evil perpetrations
that we hide
and we can only hide
in our rolls
and in our weight
and in hiding our fear
within the crevasses
around our plastered smiles
and in between the
lines of what lies we've spate
to help others
feel comfy
and cozy amongst the quaint
dispositions
and fearful ammunitions
that fuel and feed
this world
so full of hate

BAIT

PATTERNS

we all come out
prepared to handle
a certain amount

but if we stretch too far
a distance
in too short
a time
it can cause
anxiety

and if we fail to reach
what we think we can handle

– fail to fulfill –

a preconceived spectrum
we may come to experience
depression

will I ever be able
to love myself enough
to heal all the pain in my heart

all the suffering I've chosen
and let tear me apart

IT FEELS LIKE A LOSING BATTLE

I've been to the bottom
where the bottom dwellers dwell
where they feast off the doubters
and the singed – winged folks from hell

I've looked death
and the urge for going
right between the eyes
and cried out a most mournful
bloody
soulful cry

I have felt nothing

and do you know what that is like

it's dormant
it's lonely
strangely freeing
and hopeless
it's annoying
yet comforting
to feel so lonely
when you're not alone

like roses
floating
atop the frozen arctic

with no way home

all the things
that I once
held to for hope
have gone
and here I sit
not even any need
to fight for survival
no purpose
no role
I fit
so
here I sit
without reason

yet alive

living
breathing
talking
observing

is this living

HALLOW

I'm gonna take your balls
and your dick
and wrap 'em up
around a stick
I'm gonna roll em up
then twist 'em round
and see where you're at
then
maybe
you won't make a sound

also nothing will change
because your manhood
is already
nowhere
to be found

PREJUDICE

POST-ITS

you can leave your comments
on post – its on my door

I am sorry for you but
I'm not listening anymore

I am human
a series of excuses
fake
and real
and I get excited to feel
over nothing at all

I am
running

out of excuses and
running

away from what I've known
that's failed
or succeeded
just enough to
get me by

I may be lost
but I am not gone

nor
am I . . .

FORGOTTEN

I wanted something
something to remind
remind me of who
of whom I really am

so that someday
if I think I'm someone
someone that I'm not
I'll have something
something to remember me by

HORCRUX

I tried to take my loneliness
out of my chest
and put it on the shelf
for someone else to assess

IT DIDN'T WORK

little girls
play games with love
tuning their hearts
to the next bite
of happiness
– the spark –
however forgetting
all those whom
they've left
in the dark

ALIVE

tears slowly graze
from the outside corners
of my eyes
down my blushed cheekbones
making their way

white hatch marks on a
pink plate

they always choose to
settle
in the drums of my ears

– these tears –

weave their way
through the folds and crevices
that collect what I
could not comprehend
but my body
could emote on command

bottling emotions
causes a brewing
yeast ensuing
sugars stretched
to where
upon opening
begins a foaming
of the mouth
a tightness
in the chest

RELEASE

a woman
configuring herself
in the confines of
society is a woman living
with limitation

OUTLIERS

I could lie
so you love me more
I could

I could lose
if I tell the truth
I could

the whole truth
may be too much
for your tender
hoping heart

too much
for our tender spark
to bare

or do I
underestimate
the bond
of you and I

the options for
us to try

DOORMAT

I've become such an illusion
in my own eyes
that I no longer go anywhere
without this disguise

in a constant state of stage fright
people pleaser that I am

he called my bluff
late one winter night
and I still haven't forgiven him
for seeing through my veils
and calling me out
on my shit

disgusting he once called me
it rings in my brain
and echoes in my ears
disgusting he once called me
and it makes it so frightening
to stay awake and face my fears
disgusting he called me
for my lack of loyalty
to our love

he'll never be able
to take back that word

it echoes
through the halls of my subconscious
reminding me how
the one
I sleep next to
won't play
in any
of my reindeer games

MY GENERATION

drama is
the choice drug
of the richest generation
with the most student debt
lowest payment ratings
and most emotional trauma

how rich
in drama
poor in soul
sucking from the teat
of the others

the ones already empty but
who love
to put on
a good show

I must look at my to do list
five hundred times a day
and now I'm starting to realize
that it's really just a game
that I play
with myself
to act productive
and to make myself feel
like I'm more than just
what I've constructed

who I am
has never inspired me
so much
as who I could be

STRIVING

I'm under control
in the holding cell
don't tell my man
it got me again

I wipe the canvas clean
then turn my head and it's stained again

immersed in this darkness
bright as the moon
I'm still as stone
locked in my tomb

held there
wailing for you
stuck without a prayer
a suck with no chew

as scorpions stretch
the poison from my breast
the clutch of sadness
I cannot resist

I wipe the canvas clean
then turn my head and it's stained again

TRENCH

I watch
as kids try to catch
the lies they've been told
in rivers and streams
with butterfly nets
while the lie
tellers
sit to the side
rigidly
ridiculing
the seekers
innocent
of adventure

I look down at my legs
from an angle
no one ever sees

my skewed perspective
of myself
is messing with my mind
as I try to appease

I'm tired of the
trigger warnings
and topics
deemed taboo

life is a trigger
and you're the only one with
the determining finger

I never thought to consider
what he might think of me
in the end

I only ever
thought of
what I wanted in the
moment
fulfilling it
and trying to transcend

I never paused to wonder
or think about
how my actions would affect
his affection

not until
the very end

SELFISH CONSIDERATIONS

maybe

I'll just let
the darkness
take me this time

I will not lose
this battle with sadness

I will not allow
sadness to steal
the ocean inside me
with these tears

VICTORY

death can come
I am ready
for I refuse to suffer
any longer

REBIRTH

somewhere

in

between

I really didn't think

I would ever make it out
of the darkness

at least not alive

[I THINK I DID]

well

if my own drama
didn't destroy me

I guess
nothing will

these tiger stripes
I've earned
help to break the fall
of biting the dust
at every turn

STRETCH MARKS

I was so busy
looking at the fallen tree
that I didn't notice
the bump in front of me

AWARENESS

I was too ignorant
to shatter
the illusions
I ended up cocooned within

DELUSIONS

I am a reflection
of the mother
of our planet

so often
I find myself
tearing at the earth

and
though I don't quite know why
I know it hurts

I KNOW THE HURT CAN HEAL

I protect myself from the elements
every day with these clothes

but at the end of the day
the elements
are what I need most

and the clothes are just getting in the way

BARRIERS

LIMINAL

I want to be this
undefined character
that fits in between
all the spaces
of descriptive words

separating myself
from the images
I see
of others

I'm pms–ing

I can tell

I can feel my pelvis
dripping
with emotion

SHEDDING

women are like snakes
we shed our inner skins
the scales we hope
for health's sake
don't clot
and the trails left behind
we hope for
no one to notice
despite what we spit to
the media and inter-webs

women are like cattle
the way you attempt to herd us
yet we remain unheard
unabsorbed
like a super tampon
or extra-large sponge
on a light day

women are like beasts
in that we are wild
we cannot be tamed
of our natural desires

women are like kangaroos

in all of our multitasking
carrying children where we can
so we have the freedom of our hands
for other means

women are like men
like children
and all creation
we connect and fuel each other
in the blank spaces
where we find one another
and hold hands to barricade
from those who herd and shame us
but who are truly jealous
of our gift of renewal
each month

becoming familiar with
pain
more and more
each month

I learn a new lesson
from a trial I face
to make me stronger

mostly
in the face of
myself

STRONGER

are you getting a big head

I know I tell you you're attractive
all the time
but just because I find you
attractive
doesn't mean everyone else will
so stay with me
just
don't leave me
you can't leave me

INSECURITIES

how do I just hide it away
and then say
hey now it's time
to come out to play

my soul cannot take
this tug of war
between authentic and fake
for the sake of good rapport

JUST BECAUSE SOMETHING IS STATED
IN ALL CAPS ON A BACKGROUND
DOESN'T MAKE IT FACT

BE CAREFUL WHAT YOU OWN

these are
no longer a girl's hips
but a woman's

when did that happen
where
was I

did it happen overnight
did it happen one cycle
one month
one moon

or when

who does this make me
now

A WOMAN

kids play pretend –
adventures
they'll grow up to have
they shout
ah the water!
watch out for the snakes!
and turn swings into ships
then grow up to sit at desks
the adventure – dreams
lost
in their starched collars
and trouser seams

maybe you can never be ready
for when your children break your heart
maybe they have to really break it
in order for evolution to occur
and both parties to grow into themselves
as individuals

you cannot be illuminated
without a shadow
following you

it moves
ever
with us

sharing in
in our stride

never alone
our shadow
stands there beside us
beneath us
supporting us
and questioning our
self – assurance
from the inside
out

SHADOW SELF

I'm not so brittle
or sensitive as I may seem

don't discount me
just because I live in dreams

ELASTIC

IRONING

you pick fights with me
when you're feeling low
do you think you'll feel better
after we have a row
completely induced by you
and your personal doubts
but do you really have to shout
at me so fiercely
and break apart
my penchant for the arts?

boy, do we have
a lot of work to do...

I didn't know I had any
buttons to push
until you held them all down
refusing to let up
even as I yelled
and fought against
the pressure

now there's no buttons left
and although I hated you
for a time
I'm now quite grateful
for the clarity
of mind
and lack of useless
baggage
that had
for so long
plagued my
internal paradigm

BAGGAGE

TURN

I didn't leave
because of something
you didn't give me

I left because
I found something
too beautiful
to turn away from

man if I could
I would
go back in time
say hello to you
kiss you
call you mine
and never ever
look back again

HINDSIGHT

SOUL MATES

I still love every soul mate
that I have ever known
even whilst not residing
so deep within these bones

eternal threads of courage
may link me to you
but no matter how I forage
I can't seem to see straight through

I'll stay away completely
for that's this life's true path
but just know dear how confusing
it can all be in the aftermath

I use the blood
to season the meat

training the human body
to digest muscles

bringing myself
closer to vampirism

COOKING

which came first

the education system
or my anxiety

THE CHICKEN

the circles are getting darker
underneath our eyes

as a collective
as a world

the poisons are
coming out

we're so in need
of a detox
to our systems

it's beginning to show

in the shadows
like quicksand
we are caught

and all we can see
through our blindness
is the onslaught
of empathy

empathy

what on earth is empathy

we're all so caught up
in consoling
the sensitivity
but I wonder

if that kindness we lend
just protects others from
bending their own rules
and acting outside themselves
like they know deep down they want to

if the people of a society
weren't so intent on fitting a box
around themselves
to feel held and contained by the support
of predetermined fates
then perhaps other people wouldn't
be deemed crazy when
they don't
or can't fit
a box around themselves
too

allowing
emotions to
constantly cater
to sensations
leaves one
in a state of
eternal reaction

RESPONSE

I'm not ready to look back

not yet

sometimes
the darkness of my memories
still consumes me

TRIGGERS

I'm evolving so quickly
I can't keep up
my voice is in constant
discussion with itself
so how do I say anything
when it's all passing through
flowing out like magma
never settled
never cool

sometimes I find
that I'm speaking my mind
through a public vocabulary
that was passed down
through time

if just fulfilling the spaces
in between each lip
and allowing learned
sounds and patterns of
words to escape

automatically
without a second thought
from what my subconscious
was taught

LEXICON

dear laughter:

permeate my angry bones
rattle my conscious aggression
and turn the coin
to the sun
on this
incessant repression

a wick won't light
when wet
my soul won't ignite
when kept

and I can't fight
if I
can't find the light

ILLUMINATION

I can bend the page
with my pen

sculpt it in new ways
now and then

sometimes
these pages even
write themselves
making use of the leftover ink
from my emotional daze

INK

I'm trying not to carry around anger
but it clings to my eyelids
– an every time stranger –
no matter where I look

it's just me
and my anger

left smacking lips
at the world
as we see fit

S T U C K

there exists
always
the potential
for joy

you just
have to shift
to see where it sits
inside

SEARCH

our hearts
are portals
to infinite love

if you can't find love
look there

(for you'll never
find it
in your mind)

no one
can validate
your self – growth
for you

NOT EVEN YOU

I need a deep connection

a place to bury my soul
someone who understands me
whom I can love without control

BURY ME

we've been warned since our youth
of the troubles she brings
when she arrives
to wash out and cleanse the
fears and troubles that get caught
where we feel
and grow ties

when she comes
she comes like a torrent
to take our troubles
and wring them dry
of wrinkles where they don't belong
and to clear the cosmic skies

this softest part of us
holds the harshest emotions

FIRST BLOOD

I cannot hold onto anything in this world
including myself

who I am today may not be
who you meet tomorrow

I refuse to keep myself similar
or keep constant
for your comfort

nature doesn't explain itself
and neither shall I

for I am the elements
a constantly evolving combination
of collaborations and correlations
of the microscopic

BLEND

METAPHOR

there's a safety in metaphor

it eases communication
across the board
and helps us stay comfy
when we've gotta cut it to the core

you've helped me

overcome fears
that may have otherwise
consumed me

yet

you're the reason
I first let them in

ARE THANKS IN ORDER

I don't want to walk around
with complimentary – induced
confidence
clipping my sovereign heels

rather
I want to find
a prowess
completely devoid
of ego

STILL SEARCHING

I cannot forget
no matter what I do
that my journey is for me
and I am not you

WHAT'S GOOD FOR THE GOOSE

just because something worked for you
doesn't mean it will work
for anyone else
we are not the purveyors of the universe
we are merely here
to purvey our own experience
in human form
and cross-pollinate the stories
of what we learn

O N E

it's safer
to just stay inside

I can't cause anything
if I stay inside

FAILURE

how many droplets
make up the ocean
and we just lump
them together
calling them
the sea

do they not deserve
a bit more credit
for their impeccable teamwork?

OCEANIC SPREE

it took me three years
of mourning
to see that it wasn't really
you I missed at all
but a part of me
that left when you did
and became instantly forgotten

REFLECTIONS

NOSTALGIA

the nostalgia
like an anchor
roots me to where
I no longer belong

SALVE

mothers are
devil's advocates
to their daughters
defining their worst fears
by the judgements they
lovingly apply
like salve to their child's chest
afraid of becoming
a witness
to what they've worked so hard to
avoid for themselves

I go to the laundromat
cause I can't afford the casino

I love sliding change
in slots
and hearing the ding
as it passes through the machine
and the coins begin to
sing

PAVLOV

I am but a part of her journey
where
she is the root of mine

MAMA

here we go again
trying to list off
what we are
how we define ourselves and
what we need
to be happy

really we've only come
to this point of lists
for a false kind of confidence
that we fill ourselves with
as we shuffle through it all

I need sunshine
you need rainfall
but really didn't we say
we'd only need each other

HORRORS

the hush
of a downpour
reminds me
of the horrors
we create
with our hearts

I had a nightmare
my nipples were gone
and it taught me how
I don't want my
daughters
or my sister's
daughters
growing up
with heads
filled with as many
I'm not enough's
as I've had to fight through
the years

TEAR THE PAST TO SHREDS

the wars
we wage
with ourselves
write the conflicts
of our world

WE WRITE OUR HISTORY

sometimes I find
and peel off
bits of your dried cum
on my skin
the children we
aren't having
the fights we don't
even begin

BLOOM

I've been making myself out
to be something special
but like everybody else
I'm searching for a voice
just something to say
every day
so they don't all feel like a waste

I'm always
so confused
by the (as to the)
parameters
to which (by which)
we're playing

GAMES

silence
like an atomic bomb

the notes flew away
extended in space

explosive
the tones were all frozen
and hung in the air

clinging
as though unaware
of the moment they would remember

a memory now
ingrained in a frequency
of despair

THE ANNOUNCEMENT OF ILLNESS

we're retrogrades of each other
mirroring opposites
– magnets –
you travel to me
and I follow you back
teeter totter

two swings in synch
moving in motion
not unlike that silver – balled
mechanism that's supposed to
calm you down
and so it does

S O D O Y O U

upon bleeding no more
there's wisdom in store
though I've battled it with fear
and disgust
looking to my elders
and wanting to truly be forever young

but that would be choosing
the life of the fool
the sight of one who
sees not the truths
as they come

AGING

I am a woman in the world
and walk into a woman's room
to do what I have to do
I pee and bleed and shit and wash
withdrawing for those times
when I am in between
being lost and unseen
gently resisting beside your naked eye
never resting
so long as you find me unclean

R I V A L R Y

why are we so afraid
of our own darkness

why do we exorcise it
extricate it
and expel it
rather than find out what it wants
and why

getting to know your darkness
can feel like
finding a best friend
that you come to understand
and may even envelop in the end

DARK MIRROR

I spent so much time
thinking
how much you were like me
that I forgot
to get to know you

SELFISH LOVE

WARRIORS

my cigarette and I
are warriors together
in a world
that wants us to run

in circles
dizzy from the race
for invisible treasures
forgetting what our souls touch

but we refuse
to forge anything
that isn't pure

always so many thoughts
rattling round
in this strange little brain

s t r a n g e
as non–normative
strange
as a compliment
strange
as deranged
strange
as not caged

UNBOUND

our emotions sculpt our memories
and I look back on mine with you
with dust behind my water – logged gaze
twinkling in the limelight of the truth

SCULPTOR

I am not a picky poet
I don't mind
a simple rhyme
nor an esoteric retreat
from the norm
of a form

but what I mind
and cannot commend
is when
I feel nothing
and am bored by the end

this is not so much judgement on
either the poet or myself
but more a dread
I find in place
of something more intriguing
of tone
meaning
meter
and
time

CREASE

these rolls
fold
on my
body
now
they crease
my skin
and a belly swell
sits off to the side
growing
waiting
asking
for some attention
some stimulation
of the area
but I'm not ready
to face the emotions
sitting inside there
just yet

not ready to release
what got stuck
inside of my emotional
net

I am inspired by chaos
but bored
by the still

I'D BE MORE PRODUCTIVE THE
OTHER WAY ROUND

one day I'll tell you why

one day

when I think you believe me
again

PACING THE DAYS

you have to feel
the flames of a fire
to learn how to tame it

COCOON

does a butterfly remember itself
after it comes out of its cocoon

does it remember all those lonely nights

does it miss what it knew
or rejoice
in what's new

I pull fits from the furnace
and I'm not proud
but I have love

DETERMINED

he is
who he is

I am
who I am

and so
how we exist
is in
how we combine

shift out of your pride
shift it all aside
and
soften

surrender yourself
to the memory
of patience

tough love
is so soft
under your touch

DELIGHT

when we first met
my heart held disdain for you
and yet
and yet we fell madly in love

so tell me why
tell me how
love can work this way

where the distaste of
chocolate under my tongue
becomes my most favorite delight

the scent
has left
from under my nose
it lingers
awhile
each time we go
away
from one another
but it's getting stronger
with every passing trace

YOUR SMELL

REMORSE

what if
some day
someone banned what you love
and the majority followed

would you finally feel
remorse
for how you killed what others love
with your closed mind and
hardened heart

words
like fibers
get lost

swept away
by a current
a breeze

insignificant
unless strung
together

I struggle with the pacing
of life
I never know when to act
when to fight
and when to let go
and allow

it seems
I always allow
when I should've acted
and
you guessed it
acted when I should've
stayed on the couch
smoked a joint
and snacked

FLUCTUATIONS

I am a piece of music
with my weight
speed
and energy
changing
fluctuating
ebbing
and flowing
with time

S P U N

the new moon inches closer
as does my own time

yet another layer
sheds itself
away from
my mind

stripped down
over and over
to the basics
of what remain

full moon
and full moon again
such a powerful gift
this is

this ability
to renew
and reawaken myself
inching ever closer
to my most authentic nature

I feel
the energy swelling
tides rolling in
to strip away my already shed skin

and dissolve it

in the salt of the seawater

which was

once

the tears

I shed

over a skin

that no longer fit

MOON TIME

BENIGN

stones and bones make stories
foretold by the glories
our ancestors made

world – worn whispers
rattle our breath
while our own
throat – sung melodies
silence the benign
to its chilled death

is it the world that's changing
or is it me

SISTERS TO THE SAME DEMISE

it's reminding yourself
that you're walking through green pastures
when all you see are peat bogs
surrounding your feet

TRYING TO BE HAPPY

understanding
can sometimes be
the most limiting thing
of all

LIMITATIONS

surrender to the suffer
in order to heal

SURRENDER

nothing lasts

just as these words
are
but embers in a fire
soon to be swept away

fumes of a mutable domain

solutions of vapor
sucked through a flame

ALL THESE WORDS

you're my fire
my flame
the wild thing inside
I hope to never tame

requite my love
requite my desire
and help me tame the fear
I refuse to inspire

TWINS

memories dissolve
like cotton candy
on my tongue
as I freeze myself
like a camera
steadying to snap
trying to hold a memory
– an image –
in its grasp

DREMA

the chronic disappointment
and
eternal guilt
don't fuel me anymore

I refuse
to feed off of them
or respond
to validate
the game

like a rabid dog
I had my addictions
to guts
to gore
to feeling
spiritually sore
and alienating myself
from the wild wolf woman
waiting ashore

BUT I'M CHANGING

justice
in the name of love
is compassion
he said
staring
with that
intense flame
he always carries

wow
I wish my thoughts
were so eloquent
so beautiful
I said
while
wondering if I would
be the success
or the failure

DIFFERENT TEAMS

misty morning mysteries
fill this winter woman
when nothing else
is quite alive

she walks through snow paths
treks along ridges
across what once were rivers
and will be again

her inner wildfire
contently fueling her desire
all kept at bay
for the sake of safe survival

this winter woman
can't whisper her secrets
for they'll freeze solid
in the snow

this winter woman
is she lonely
she doesn't know
(she'd never ask herself)
she just moves ahead
as she will
until
her very last breath

DRAWN

like the ocean
you're drawn to her
and don't know why

she pulls you under
can't even help it
that's just her tide

you can't fight it
can't do anything
but hope
only hope
she carries you to a
new shore
taking you far from where
you were before

the silence is screaming
it's so unloved

HEARTBURN

no longer
do I live
in a hypochondriatic horror

FINDING PEACE WITHIN DEATH

EMOTION OCEAN

I know

at those moments

I'm talking through water
always through water
head down
brows furrowed
arms overhead
barreling through the flames
to find some
emotions I recognize
to mold to carve to
a walking stick to ground to
the earth as I walk
and as the dust fills my throat
and the air whips the heat up my shoulders
I attempt to clear it
struggling to cough it all up
then finding blood
and water
always water
flooding my mind
my face
and my pride

the helplessness floods too
riding the wave of that
emotion ocean
so that all my words
no matter how well chosen
come out liquid
and manifest this helplessness
that I perceive
as open

I want to
embody
an ecstatic
aesthete
adventuring
abound

G O A L S

take a moment
in the day to day
to listen to what
the trees have to say

their mother
is dying
because of our greed
and how we
have poisoned
her every seed

WE TOOK ADVANTAGE

I didn't do it
the way you wanted me to
but I did do it
knowing how
every day
I was waking up
to your disappointment
by choosing my way
instead of the pathway already paved

THIS IS STRENGTH

sometimes
you're like sandpaper
and I can't speak
through the stridence
of your rasp

COARSE

every expectation
everything we're *meant* to do
is only a distraction
a smokescreen
to keep us busy
so we don't see
the greater truth

P L O Y

sometimes I hear the call
of Mother Nature
come back to me
my child
she whispers in the wind
find me in my rivers
and on the top of my mountains

I'm coming momma
I whisper back
with the movement of my body
harsh and quick
beating my bones on her dirt
heart pounding like one
expansive
drum

HOUL

I am not my emotions
or at least not entirely
rather I can pick and choose
if I want to allow the feelings to
permeate past my internal blues

no longer
will the waves crash
upon me
the hapless
helpless
victim

N O L O N G E R

just don't
let it
overwhelm you

THE BEST ADVICE I EVER RECEIVED

there's a whole
ocean in me
trying to get out

it flows all around
in there
causing pressure
behind the eyes
at times

and it seems
I can't control
what flows out
in the overflow
of the overwhelm

AN OCEAN BEHIND THE EYES

SLIP

I try to remember
that healing isn't linear
whether it's
emotional
spiritual
physical
mental
whatever

but then
I have a bad day
and
slip myself
down the first drain
I meet

falling into my despair
that I'm not whole yet
that I'm not quite there

forgetting completely
that the process
is never linear

somewhere between
shadows and light
self-love and hate
is where I seem
to exist

between
reality and dreams
illusion and fact
is where
I find myself

where disillusionment dissolves
as ash in a pool of water
and truth stretches
like slime

I wait for my own resolve
to find me
and capture my spirit
in a blaze of conscious sublime

my current goal:
to be a woman without
without baggage
without fear
with balance and strength
and creativity in spades
in folds
and carried along the blades with which
she ferociously sculpts her
precise life
not without surprise and change
as these constants will without
and without which I cannot
exist
and with enigmatic moment to moment
love drenched
word pressed
fear ridden
magical feats
of fortitude and calm strength
a woman wild in her wisdoms
and smiling freeness
a woman river
carrying a current through her life
adept at flowing through
creating ripples and rough rapids
to navigate any
and all terrain

I fell out of my own heart
and jumped right into yours

WE ALL LIVE DIFFERENT PLACES

my terrain changes
sometimes with the weather
always with time

CURVES

with hyena breath
I cackle
in the face of my
fears

scraping the sides of the world
with the crest of my tongue
my thighs beating and writhing

two great drums

to the touch of a wounded
throng
amidst an everlasting song

and the creases of
my face
and my yoni
feel the longing
for the resounding
gong

FINDING CONFIDENCE

my hair's gotten
so long
since I've seen
you last
and though we talk
on the phone
it just doesn't show
the truth
to the times
that pass

DISTANCE

I want to lead women back to their own knowing
I want to help women find their path
I want to help humans find one another

men find patience and kindness in the pain of their growing
women grace and strength when their ways are tested

and in each of us
in each of our souls
the journey back
to our innate wisdoms

I hope this to be a real adventure
I hope you find every element enticing
from the struggles and tribulations
the world lay at your feet
to the peaks and triumphs you find
in the moments of joy you seek

survival in strength and endurance
survival in the essential enigmatic
and the drive to thrive
spread publicly
through every word you speak

sometimes I look back
at myself
in photos from months ago
and see
those people are not me
we are not one
more just someone I was once
close to
and now
I'm different cells
different feels
different clothes
different smells
too much change for us to be one
and yet
I'll make an album of some
of the people I was before
and look back
tearfully
at the
timestamp
really the only testament
to the fallen trees
of the forest
inside me

she calls them spells
for
even the most painful
and uncomfortable
of experiences
are rooted
in magic

S E I Z U R E S

RISE

I am a slayer to myself
just a pawn
a player
in the game
I was shown

I rise with the wind
and descend at dawn
sipping the flavors
like a complacent fawn

bleeding the feeding
selling the tome
you've got your interests
at heart
and I've got my own

slay the
denominations
inside

the demons
that still
try to hide
and reckon with the self

that clings to survive
amongst the claw teeth
and blood – drawn eyes

I'm nicest to myself
when I'm fed

and funny enough
it comes easiest when
I've bled

when the water and smoke
clear

there's only myself
to fear

the hawks soar overhead
like spiritual vultures
waiting for my awakened soul
to surge on up and
follow their lead
down the spaceless
timeless path
that has freed me
once before
let the joy overthrow
the fear and fill
the buckets of hate
with love
and while I'm up there
up above
remember to call
connect and
(something that rhymes with love)

SOAR

so many
people
drag their bodies
around
as they navigate
the terrain
but
not me
no
I will hold myself with honor
integrity
and trust
trust in myself
in the universe
within which I exist
and trust in those I
share my light
– my life –
with

A PLACE I WANT TO TAKE YOU

it's only you
who could turn
my shriveled
wooden heart
into a spectacle
of art

LATHE

think of the hours
mama
think of how much time
of our lives
mama
we got to share
how much quality time
with one another

think of the day trips
the traffic frustrations
the shopping
the cooking
the laughing
over your silly perceptions of the world
mama

or mine

I miss you every day
mama
my best friend
my closest ally

I miss telling you all my secrets
and forcing you to triple promise
not to tell
but then I knew you'd always tell

somebody

I miss cooking in the kitchen
mama
and laughing raucously at my doing all the work
while you chop one carrot
mama
I miss you solving all my problems
mama
I'm not ashamed to admit it
I hate having no one to whine to anymore
mama
unless you call
but then I have to hear all about your day
when all I wanna do is whine
mama

I miss your eye contact
mama
and the way you always listened to me
and remembered what I shared with you
unless it was something I just said
mama
then we know you'd ask two more times
for me to repeat
cause you were actually daydreaming
mama
I miss calling out to you

MOM
mama
and having you shout right back
WHAT

and I miss worrying about you
and taking care of you
when you needed me to
cause that's how much I love you
my momma

I love you mom

are you listening
mama

I should have a recorder
taped to my inner thoughts
so that so many good words
don't all just wash away
like they did today

T A P E

still haven't sold our souls
and this ain't how it normally goes
but we make it
we make it

like the stories our folks foretold
we lived the pain but choose to stay
and work on what we've got
to say

cause it's so beautiful
loving you
so far beyond what I thought I knew
and it's all because of you
your patience
your heart
– the effort –
that I know we'll make it through

I miss
the smells
the way my hair stands on end
with electrocuted delight
the arches
my body builds
in an attempt towards flight

I miss
the shutoff
of my hyper – aware self
and the awakening
to the depths
of something
something else

I miss
the imprints
your fingertips leave on my skin
and the bumps
when
(oh, my)
it raises in attempt
to reach for what's held deep within

I miss
your lips
and the way we cascade ours

all over
the landscapes
of one another's
form

I WISH YOU WERE HERE

not only is finding yourself
as a woman in the world
a near impossible task
but simply understanding
how to find yourself
as a human
in the current
of the moment
is like plucking a fish
from a river

will we choose the right path
when we've only a moment to choose

will we get plucked by the right searching hand
or will we fall prey to another's feast

will we swim
or get caught up and lost
in the currents
that cut us
to our most innate
cut us truly
to our core

RECENT FINDINGS

this is my blood

my body

the most religious experience
I could ever get my spirit on

I watch
the way
the blood absolves
my fears of springing a leak

I watch it absorb
into the skin of my fingers

no trace of worry
in my wise eyes

the way I contort
not for others' comforts
but for my own wacky ways

wanting to groan
and mourn

this life not gifted
it's not the time
not now

not yet

but when it is
I'm ready
confidently rising
to each occasion
answering each call
I hear ring

the echo
the pump
of the
blood of my
veins

the veins woven
by
my womanly ways

A TASTE OF DEATH

LIGHT

I've lived so many lives
shed so many skins
and yet
I still begin
each time
with love

THE START

I took a light step
towards an inferior dark
with trust in my heart

and found
as soon as I
passed through
the gate
veil
portal
passageway
divide
that what I had perceived as the dark
was only a moment of blindness
before I found myself
squinting
with new eyes
into the light
of a great white sun

for
fresh eyes
present the opportunity
to resolve
all conflict
relieve
all tension

somewhere in there
I became a woman

READY

no speculum
member or
foreign tower
shall ever again
sever the tie
between
my clit and I

WILDNESS

I was once so attached to the idea
that I was wild

I clung to it
clawed my own skin away
to keep it

when real wildness found me
freedom came with it
and I found
they had already been there all along

resting
beneath my
perceptions
waiting
for the control
to cease

my breasts were but buds
when I called them blooms

shifting peaks
now calling in more room
or calling to the tomb
I can't tell
they rise and fall
with my tides

we might call them majestic
though they're barely
more to feel
we're just playing by the daylight

by the heat these skins can feel

there is history
in the grains
of my pain

passed down
through the veins
that carry the blood
of my
mothers and
mothers
and mothers

ANCESTRAL

I will be strong
a strong woman

unafraid of the shame
guilt
or blame
that come from going against the grain

GRAINS OF THE SAME SAND

being blood and blood
and blood alone
unlocked the lips
that revealed the smiles
laughter
and stories from living
loving
giving
so full of love

and yes I was
invited in

into this lightness
by blood

LINEAGE

can you feel my heart
when it beats for you

TOGETHER OR APART

the right decisions
are the ones
you make
for yourself

NOT TO RELY ON OTHERS

every
day
reminding myself
that it's okay
to remember now
no more are the days of forgetting
to survive
now is the time to blossom
and recall
that once upon a time
you remembered things well
and now
you can again

IT IS SAFE

like a bridge
gratitude
can span the gap
from sorrow
to joy

now

that darkness in darkness
eventually
called me towards the light
but you will never know
my struggle
as I crawled and scratched my way
through the black of that dark night
and slowly peeled back
the layers
of repression
that had clouded up my sight
and learned to love
to love myself with intention
to love with indignation and self-preservation
and with the power of the cycles
that are so inherently fem(inine)
to aid me in my plight

DYSPLASIA PT. II

a year spent
slowly tearing
away
from the important places
within

REATTACH

at the touch of love
a warrior
is born

FOR PLATO

we chose to be together
to be the perfect challenge
for each other's tendencies
taking us closer to our
fully found selves

HALVES OF THE OTHER

GROWTH

you escape
the scope
of future hopes
by holding on
to what you know

executing
future truths
for fear of losing
what you're used to
what you've been through
and hold close to
through all the moments
shrouded in doubt

why not instead
allow what's changed
to take effect
take a deep breath
look around
and witness a new truth
you just grew into

all the courses in the world
couldn't have taught me
what our love has

SCHOOLED

you're a boat
and I am the ocean

will you make it to shore
or will I swallow you whole

just don't stop sailing
across my seas

no matter how rough
the waters may seem

I'VE GOT YOU

BRISTLES

your voice sounds sweet on my ears
I swear I met you before

skin softly bristles on mine
how I remember you later

I come like no one's watching
even when we're only talking
darling

there exist so many ways
I have moved my body
lips
tongue
pussy

and so many ways
I didn't know I could
until you

TEACHABLE

the clouds hang
in the air
– they cling –
like your fluid on my skin
in the mornings
all the mornings
when you convince
my form
to breathe open
and allow
for our love
to enter in

H I G H - S T R U N G

the only man
able to calm the hungry winds
that have taken so many people's sins

since back before the world was touched by blood

is the only man
who braved the storms
I set to his soul
out of fear and remorse
then patiently
waited
for me
while I
taught myself
how to love freely

LIKE THE WIND

if you're ever tired
if you're ever cold
you can sleep inside me
I'll keep you warm

LEARNING HOW TO LOVE

the kind of light
that makes your ears
squint

HOW IT FEELS WHEN WE TOUCH

SUNSET

may you
never again
go a sunset
without knowing how much I love you

every border
is imagined

color without lines

CHILD'S PLAY

salted caramel blowjob

the best
and when you
put on too much
we giggled
leading to more comfort
more intimacy
more empathy
and a greater finish

CARAMEL

I am a
stay at home jedi
fighting problems
with my pen

my voice is
– our voices –
are what ignite
the flames of
evolution

WHY I WRITE

only in letting go
can we
truly possess
what is real
for
it has to snow
for the flowers to grow
up once more
in spring

I would like your whole heart to live in
confide in
build within
work with
strengthen
take from
knead like dough
need like the sun
shimmer through
find myself in
you are the everything

I want
to inhale you in the mornings
and let you fill up my lungs
breathing you into my toes
and the tips of
the nails on my fingers
the top of my shoulders
and the crown of my head
and when I should need to exhale
I exhale all the bad
and keep you inside
giving me life
you and the bourbon
and the dead sea salt baths

I continue to grow in love
by the light of your fire
I promise to stoke the flames
and keep your brightness alive

see you in the mirror
having my back
and welcome your visions
into view
to shatter the illusions
I once thought I knew

I ' V E G O T Y O U

I am the weaver
of my world
stringing ideas
emotions
and experiences together

when they taught me to walk
I started to dance
they said speak
but all I did was sing
the poet
when they gave me a pen

the sculptor when they gave me wood
from a fallen tree
or herbs to make tea

even embers and cinder I pressed
into diamonds

and when I foraged for more
I found a wood that was petrified
scared in its slow death
pressure and time
it's only life steps

TOOLS OF NATURE

I am a wildflower child
of the moon
the sun
and mother
of all creation

Thank Goddess
for her
and all this green and blue

basically
we're renegotiating the past
in this history class

at some point
(at any point) in time
does the past become
– is it –
irrelevant?

TOO SOON?

I love her
I love him
I love
her
I love him
I love him
I love her
I. love. her.
and my lover
too

FAMILY

I've got this little family
and we sometimes intertwine
all our little heart beats
in a rhythm
in time

INTERTWINE

let your children be the
only ones
who tame you

let them carry your fire

I'm glad I had a one
that got away
so he could
go
get away
get gone
and leave room
for the one
I was really meant to be with
all along

I am no longer
marching through dirty waters
but gliding along
working at my own pace
in peace

my blood responds

it no longer
ails me
and asks for all my time

there is no longer

so much

such confusion
and fear to wade through

not when love wears you
like a wetsuit
and you wear it with pride
as it glides
and guides you

my emissions are clean
my heart pure love

CRESCENT

the moon wanted to hang out
too much last night
so I couldn't sleep

she wanted to welcome me
to the dawn
before my own
moon time
menagerie

we spoke about learned lessons
connected over
wisdoms
and listened to
each other's heartbeats

as well as the sound
of our breaths
deep
and proud
each so
prideful
and full
to know the other
and come to connect so close

at this time
each month

sisters
in crescent
though not in flesh

what is a lover

what is found
what is seen

is a lover a witness

such as

is

a

poet to her
own thoughts

the chill of winter
stills my strive
as it calms the achiever
and awakens the inner feeler

love never ends
and it doesn't die
it exists forever
in the beholders eye

you carry the stories of your
ancestors
on your lips

speak your story
aloud
when you feel aroused

for
your wisdoms need only the
spark of alignment
to be shared through your experiences

FORETOLD

break the titles
and labels
from our lips
and
leave our hips
out of it

WOMB-MEN

round and round
we bend
for one another's light
to be held upright

CONTINUUM

their outstretched hands
healed wounds
that went
unobserved
by the masses

THE RIPPLE

the mind is merely a

tool
for the soul

USE IT WELL

I have fallen
into and out of your arms
a thousand times over
and now
I finally
get to stay there
forever

THE MOVE

it was as though
every cell
that makes up my body
had an eyeball on it

many were open
but others were closed
and when you walked into my life
it was as though
every eyeball opened
a great yawning blink
never to need the rest again
never to sleep through this life again

not because of another but
because of a connection
between two souls
to support and to grow
from the sturdy foundation
a bountiful garden
that always had the right seeds
but never before
the right soil to sow them

SEEING CELLS

when we clasp
our hands tight
at the knuckles

we're connected and centered
as one

allowing us to
reopen together
like a pollinated flower
to the wielding world around

you and I
are why
words like
love
magic
and
chemistry
exist

they're trying to codify
something that's
un – codify – able

like you and I

your body is
a barrier for me
from the rest of the world

S T A Y

the potency of
the history
or rather herstory
of humankind
is found
in the details
of your story
and mine

SPEAK

the heart

is

the most
resilient part
of our divine
consciousness

only I can create what I see
I am the sole creator of my reality

please
dearest self
remember this:

that you pave your own path
off the visions in your head
not the perceptions and perspectives
of those who think
they know you
– could ever understand you –
better than you

you
see you
know you
love you

twenty-eight circles
around the sun
and what have I learned
what have I done

I've come to see
the true beauty inside me
and pull that outside
to share with the world

I've learnt to treat
my body well
nourish and foster
my own nature

and be true
to how I really feel
never hide it away
for that's no way to heal

I've had some scrapes
and bruises of late
that have shown me great beauty
as I rose up to satiate
my prowess
and all that I was
able to do
to define

define
and redefine
how I fit in this world
I was brought up into
to honor the self
and all its vulnerable feels
and listen to my body
mind
spirit
and what's in the details
when I take good care
of my own true nature
authenticity grows from me
flowers to spread the cure

the seeds travel far
and at times stay close to home
but all come from a place
where my true nature is known

twenty-eight turns
around the fair sun
here's where I've come
to fruition
even though
I've really just begun
I've shed the skins of innocence
that were holding me back

and brought about a cognizance
that will carry me on
to the next and next
of my circles round the sun

I've learnt the real value
of what it means to buy a dress
who it affects and what my choices say
where I disperse my earned affects
switched from indulging
in chaos
to indulging in essentials
baths and crystals
and a pisco sour now and then

though these things might not stick
they feel like the right fit
for the kind of life
I imagined

and now I've got
some new dreams I'm forming
just starting to welcome
and confide my soul secrets in

we'll see what I move towards
for decisions aren't real
just pathways

to walk down
instincts to follow
and feel

I am no label-able thing
no pixie
no feminist
no fiend

I am all of these and all of more
but no label needs to tell me of my core

twenty-eight circles
round the faire sun
and now I'm sure
of what I have become

R E A L

I'm going to
love my self
so fiercely
that love
will be the only
shield
I need

I aim to attain my heart's dreams of fluid artistic expression. I focus myself on what brings me the most pleasure, and with a joyful heart, navigate my way towards what I want. I continuously delve in more deeply to my life experience, fully aware of the beauty at hand in every moment. I accept with deep wisdoms in my mind, and root into the truth that where I am is where I am meant to be. I am full of joy and appreciation for all that transpires and will use precision in the years ahead to craft the life I desire. I find outlets for my creative fusions as the desires arise, naturally expressing myself in inspired alignment with my truest self.

A DREAM IS A PRAYER

these pages

are all that's left

merely the residue

– the embers, ash, dirt, and dust –

of a human being

a woman learning to love herself

no, really

finally, this time

learning

MARIESA FAER

storyteller and poetess
by birth
she strives in her creative actions
to focus her light
in the right directions

even through the toughest of shadows

ABOUT THE PUBLISHER

Smokeblood Publishing is a mythopoetic collective that strives to seek out, absorb and disseminate creative excellence in the written word.

"The whole thing is a weaving of smoke." -Alan Watts

If you'd like to publish your own book, or for bulk discounts, please contact the publisher directly:

IG: @_smokeblood

Email: connect@smokebloodpublishing.com

Website: www.smokeblood.com

somewhere between shadow and light
is a romantic satire of interwoven stories about family
intimate relationships
menstruation
anxiety and depression
societal patterns
cultural norms
fear and death
love
inner peace
and the quest for one's inner truth

a spectrum of one human's shifting perspective
through a growth cycle
recorded in voice

this book is a physical residue of
and tribute to
the awakening of clarity

the poems grow and expand at variant
rates from shadow to light

we each find ourselves in a variance of clarity
at differing moments in time
with differing degrees of light
through which our perceptions serve us

here lies
the etched
entrenched relief
of my journey
somewhere between shadow and light